MW01264861

Growing Up Catholic

And Getting Over It

Growing Up Catholic

And Getting Over It

William M. Nolan

Dear Matthew,

Thanks for reading this! God bless you!

Fr. Bill Nolan

VANTAGE PRESS
New York

FIRST EDITION

Published by Vantage Press, Inc.
419 Park Ave. South, New York, NY 10016

Manufactured in the United States of America
ISBN: 0-533-14969-X

Library of Congress Catalog Card No.: 2004094484

0 9 8 7 6 5 4 3 2 1

To my father, P.J., who took me fishing and taught me how to laugh and cry.

"You receive two educations in life. The first is given to you by others, and the second is the one you give yourself."

—Carter Godwin Woodson

Contents

Author's Note

Old age is a time for integrity; feeling satisfied about your past or it is a time of bitterness and despair over a wasted life. That's how Eric Erikson described the final stage of life.

This little book describes all the stages of my Catholic education and ends with the last one, integrity, gratitude and peace. Please don't be offended.

—William M. Nolan

Foreword

The human memory is a treasure-trove, a repository of sights and sounds, secrets and even smells. Hidden deep in the recesses of our minds are buried hopes and fears, unrequited dreams, doubts of old, painful unspoken hurts, bits of dirt and pernicious sins we would prefer not to unearth. Not all memories are so bleak, however, for amidst the melee flourishing in these mental groves are peals of laughter and delight refreshing our human spirits at any given moment and ratifying the sage wisdom of Shakespeare who believed that the "good that men do lives after them, the evil is oft interred with their bones." In other words, we most especially remember the good things!

In this second volume of remembrances past, author Father Nolan has revealed a host of new images from his past, the good as well as the bad. He has reported his thoughts with candor and grace, not old hackneyed thoughts from a diary or journal long ago, but fresh lively Technicolor memories which he renews and reviews in an ongoing process of an evolving self knowledge. He reaches back to the earliest happenings in his life and brings us forward to his present reflections. They become tidbits of living that we can all relate to, not cumbersome concepts too weighty to ponder.

The freshness of *Growing Up Catholic* is that it is an anecdotal look at Catholicism from inside one man's life, the lived experience of a boy, a man, a monk and a priest combined with extra experiences of being artist, poet, counselor and author. One might have called them "reflections of a disillusioned romantic" or idealist with a touch of cynicism made so by the world he sought to escape and by a church that should have known better. Moreover, this little volume is not a chore to endure, nor a mighty thesis to be proven. It is not meant to impress so much as it intends to unfurl similar reminiscences with the reader and offer compassion. It is not a competitor with the voluminous prophetic tomes being written by know-it-alls who want to showcase a vision of tomorrow's Catholic Church. Instead, this is conscience in the raw in which almost every Catholic will find some echo of his or her own faith experience; and no priest will have to strain to relate to these memories if he is as honest as the author. Father Nolan does all this in such readable and even casual manner, poking fun but making a point, weaving his story with easy wit and charm and all with masterful succinctness.

The author Virgil would look back on the travails of the past and exclaim: *"Forsan et haec alim juvabit."* No doubt the reader will be challenged to look back on his own life, remember the past once again and simply laugh.

—Father Joe Sanches

Acknowledgments

Thanks to Mrs. James L. Simmons for her generous help and patience in typing this material and offering encouragement.

Paul Schlacter, an art student at UT-Knoxville, and to William M. Nolan for executing the cartoons.

Thanks to all my friends who have been patient with me.

Growing Up Catholic

And Getting Over It

I
Growing Up Catholic

Going to Catholic School really makes you think. They throw some heavy duty things at you right off the bat. Usually a kid can just shut out stuff he doesn't understand. But when your teacher looks like a telephone booth with a face, hands, feet and a voice that seems to come from another world, you listen, even if you have attention deficit!

Being an introverted kid, I took matters seriously and pondered over all the things I heard in school. In the first grade I heard about Hell. It was an underground place where you went if you died in "mortal sin." Mortal sin is when your soul turns black. I will explain that later but now let's concentrate on Hell. Fire is what's there. If you want to know what it's like, just stick your finger in the flame of a candle. There is a clock there that says "forever, never" over and over which means "you'll never get out." The fallen angel Lucifer is in charge. He roams the world talking people into doing evil things so they will come to Hell to live with him. Everyone is screaming and howling down there. I was terrified. When I got the courage to discuss it with my mother, she said, "There's no clock in Hell, and you're not going there, so stop worrying about it." I thought to myself, *"Sister is a Bride of Christ, so she probably knows more about these things than you do."* But I didn't dare say that to my mother; I kept worrying about it quietly.

Back to sin. Sin is doing something bad. Mostly you

Can't take my eyes off of you !

know what is bad because adults tell you right away if they catch you doing it. There are little things that are bad and excusable, like getting mad, being grumpy or impolite. All you have to do is tell God you are sorry and these sins are washed away. These are called "venial sins." Big sins are called "mortals." When you do a "mortal" it makes a black stain so bad that you have to get it washed off before you die; and remember, that could be at any minute!!! You do this by going to this box in back of Church and telling the priest behind the screen what you did, if you know what to call it. "Mortals" will all be named for you as time goes by. In the meantime, I was always worried that everything was a "mortal."

The milk bottle was how Sister explained sin. The bottle is all white like your soul. Then little black spots appear. These are "venials." If you keep doing venials, pretty soon you are going to do a "mortal." That is when your milk bottle turns completely black! Then you run as fast as you can to the box with the priest in it, telling God that you are sorry all the way there. I hoped that box would be open twenty-four hours a day because I knew I would do a "mortal" sooner or later.

Although these thoughts did not keep me from learning to read and write they did distract me. I started thinking about the priest. If he could forgive you, then you wanted to stay on the good side of him. Better yet, it might be a good idea to become one! So anytime the Sister asked how many boys wanted to be a priest when they grew up, my hand shot in the air and waved vigorously. This was a nervous reaction but it sure set well with Sister!

The Last Judgment is when all the people who ever lived would stand before God to be judged and then be sent to Heaven or Hell. Each one would have all his or her sins called out by God and then each would be sent off to the ap-

This is what you don't want!

propriate place. In my mind this loomed larger than Hell itself because I knew my Mother and Dad would be there and I would be so ashamed for them to hear my secret sins. Then I heard about martyrs. That's when you die for Christ. If bad people kill you because you will not deny Christ, you go straight to Heaven! Maybe I could by-pass the last Judgment by being a martyr! Sister never asked how many wanted to be a martyr.

We practiced a lot for First Communion. Jesus was coming into my heart. He was in the little white host. One song we sang said, "Little white guest." Your heart had to be clean and white, no black spots. We wore all white. I had a little prayer book and a rosary. All this was exciting but

4

deep down I was thinking, *If Jesus is a grown-up man, how can he fit in that little wafer?* I dared not ask Sister that question. Confirmation was when the Bishop smacked you on the cheek (as my brother said), to see if you were strong enough to be a soldier of Christ.

Now that I was confirmed and growing up in the faith I decided to go over to the big Cathedral next door to our school and investigate the altar on my own. It was dark in there except for a few candles burning. I crept down the long center aisle to the golden gates before the altar, figured out how to get them open, and went to the foot of the steps of the high altar. The next move I had planned was to go up the steps to the Tabernacle and pull back the curtain and see the place where Jesus stayed. Just as I started to go up the steps two hands grabbed me from behind and I peed all over myself and all over the steps of the high altar. It was a tall Sister I didn't know. I was horrified as I peed on the high altar; this must be a "mortal." Then the tall Sister demanded to know what I was doing (besides peeing) because she knew I was up to no good. I didn't tell this sin to the priest in confession. Mother asked me why I wet my pants, I said, "I just couldn't hold it." That brings to mind the great flood.

The story of the great flood scared me. The fact that I couldn't swim might have had something to do with it. It never occurred to me that it would take an incredibly huge ship to get two of every living kind on board. It also didn't occur to me what piles of manure there would be and how bad it would smell. What stayed in my mind was a picture of those who were being swept away in the flood, and the horrible expressions on their faces. Naturally I pictured myself among the drowning victims rather than among the smug passengers on the Ark. The only consolation was that the Bible said God would never do this again! That was a relief.

5

Sacrilege?

It's only human.

Then came a scarier thought: the end of the world when everything would be destroyed by fire. The stars would fall from heaven and people would cry out for the mountains to fall on them. You never knew when it would come! Every time it stormed, my mother would light a blessed candle and we would kneel and pray before a statue of the Sacred Heart of Jesus. The hands on this plaster statue were detachable; they were each on a pin-like thing that stuck into the sleeves of Jesus. One day, when we knelt to pray during a storm, lightning hit a telephone pole and sparks flew in all directions. A clap of thunder shook the hands on the statue loose and they turned on the pins. It scared me to death. I thought, *Gabriel's trumpet sound comes next!*

Sister got all the boys together one day to talk to them about something going on in the boy's bathroom. I thought, *O Lord, it's something nasty.* There was urine on the floor every day and the janitor had to clean it up! Obviously, she didn't understand that is normal for boys to miss the target occasionally since they pee standing up and are talking and laughing. Well, she was a nun and I was sure they never had that problem in the convent.

Miracles were impossible events which happened because God wanted to manifest His power. Jesus worked them long ago, but they still happen today. Sometimes the Virgin Mary appeared to people and told them things. They were simple young people like the little peasant girl named Bernadette. I immediately thought I might be a candidate, young, poor, and simple!

One Sunday after Mass I stayed up around the Virgin Mary's altar. When I finally came out my mother was irritated and wanted to know where I had been. I said, "I was watching the statue of the Virgin Mary and hoping she would smile at me, or maybe say something." All the way home, my mother was preaching that we should not expect "special favors" from God. I sort of listened—but deep down I hoped I was still a candidate!

There were statues that cried. People dying from cancer got well instantly. We heard about all sorts of wonders but never saw any of them. There was some water available from Lourdes, France, where the Virgin Mary had appeared, and people washed in it and got well. I always kept a little bottle handy.

Holy pictures were rewards passed out by Sister. They were pictures of Jesus, Mary, Joseph, St. Theresa, St. Francis and so forth. I had a collection of these cards like other kids

No such luck! ! ! !

collected baseball cards. One day, a priest gave me an unconsecrated host. He emphasized that it was "unconsecrated," so it was just bread. It fell out of my geography book on the floor at school. Sister was horrified until I told her it was "unconsecrated" and that Father had given it to me. She was greatly relieved. She thought I was carrying Jesus around in my geography book.

It seemed like all the Saints we heard about died young. I thought, *It's probably easier to die young than it is to be holy for a long time. . . .*

Sister told us, "Never do anything by yourself that you would not do in front of your parents." That worried me until I reminded myself, *I don't go to the bathroom in front of them.* So I brushed that off.

The priest was the one who finally opened up the subject. He had all the boys in the room; apparently girls were too delicate to hear about this. He explained the sin of self abuse. It was a "mortal." He did not get down to details about how you do it, but I got the gist of it. A kid later told me that self abuse was playing with yourself. I thought to myself, *It doesn't seem like abuse to me and it's not playing either, it's serious business. Maybe he's talking about something else?* Still, if it was a "mortal," I needed to tell it in confession.

I did not know what to say in confession. What would I call it? I looked in the *Young Man's Catholic Guide* under "sins against the sixth commandment." I found "sins of immodesty." That sounded like it. After rattling off my "venials," what kind and how many times (I usually just made up the number of times because I couldn't remember), I sneaked in "one sin of immodesty."

The priest said, "Son, what do you mean by the sin of immodesty?" (The priest asking a question in confession was my worst nightmare!) So in panic, I said, "I don't know, I thought you would know." The word was in the *Young*

I thought....you would know!!

Man's Catholic Guide—surely he had read it. Later I learned that horrible, filthy, nasty word "masturbation" which I found very shameful and difficult to utter. And the act was just as difficult to avoid. So be it. At least there was confession to keep me out of Hell, if I could get there before I died.

There were also subjects that did not hit so close to home, but did cause confusion. For example, unbaptized babies who died could not go to Heaven. Original sin had not been washed away. They couldn't go to Hell; they had not committed a grave sin! *Where did they go?* They went to a place of perfect natural happiness called "Limbo." That sounded pretty good to me, sort of like Florida. But it's not Heaven! That's not fair. I couldn't believe that!

Then there was "Purgatory!" If you died with small sins on your soul you could be purified in this place so that you would be all pure before seeing God face to face. Here were those little black spots again. But I had thought they were forgiven immediately when you told God you were sorry! Yes—but even though the sins were forgiven, you still had to pay the price for the damage you had done by all your sins during your whole lifetime. That made no sense to me because hadn't Jesus already died for my sins! No one could ever explain this to me. I pictured it as a place like Hell, but you knew you get out. Now I had two things to worry about. If I dodged Hell, Purgatory would get me!

You could help the holy souls in Purgatory by making visits to the Blessed Sacrament saying prayers that had "indulgences" attached. Indulgences were like "waivers" that got you off from punishment because of some good deed you did, such as saying more prayers. You could offer up these waivers for the holy souls. That made no sense either, but it appealed to my capitalistic instinct. I felt the urge (this time a good one), to rack up tons of waivers for these souls! That meant going in and out of church over and over be-

Limbo....
The next thing to Heaven.....No adult supervision! ! !

cause they said you had to leave and come back so that each prayer was a separate visit.

You can see that strange behavior had set in. Fortunately doubt was right behind it. Speaking of strange behavior, Sister told us to make a sign of the cross every time we passed a Catholic Church in honor of the Blessed Sacrament. I used to do it when we passed any Church. When riding a bus sometimes people would look at me like they thought I had a tic or something.

Sister also told us to make the sign of the cross every time we heard someone use God's name in vain. My father was Irish and cursed a lot. My mother saw me making the sign of the cross all the time. She said, "Why are you doing

Go down two floors to Purgatory for a make over.

that?" She was probably worried about my mental health since I had mentioned wanting to see a vision. When I told her, she said, "Honey, why don't you just say a prayer for your dad each time he curses and leave off the sign of the cross?" There she was, contradicting Sister again. On the other hand whenever I was punished, Sister was always right. We also made the sign of the cross and prayed when we heard an ambulance or fire engine's siren. Maybe that's why non-Catholic kids thought we were strange.

One day a kid in the neighborhood said, "You Catholics are strange."

I said, "Yeah, some of us are; what did you have in mind?"

He said, "Do you think if I did it, I'm going to tell that I did it?" He was referring to Confession. He also told me I was not going to Heaven because I was a Catholic. Now that was a sore spot! If I didn't go to Heaven, it would be for other reasons, not because I was a Catholic. In fact, Catholics even had a special Sacrament for when you are dying, to help you get there. So all bases were covered. I gave that kid a wide berth after that.

The local priest came to the classroom once a month or so for instructions. We tried to think up impossible questions for him. Like, where did God come from? We loved to make up moral dilemmas about the "rules." The more ridiculous the better. For example, If you were on a ship that crossed the International Date Line while you were eating a hamburger and it was suddenly Friday, did you have to quit eating it? What about the mouth full you had already bitten off?

He never threw out the stock phrase "take it on faith," but usually gave us a humorous answer. We liked him.

We had been taught by Sister that you should never tell a lie for any reason. Our response was "not even to save your life?" No. "Not even to save your mother's life?" No. Not telling a lie for any reason didn't seem right! I felt it was necessary, even good, to lie sometimes. Lying is really an art! I used it now and then to make life go better for everyone!

The priest explained to us about "mental reservation" which helped with the problem. It went like this: We owe it to each other to tell the truth. We want others to tell us the truth. That's our right, since the truth affects our lives; we have the right to it. There are some things that people have no right to know. It's none of their business. He called it by a big word, "mental reservation." You can think to yourself "as far as you are concerned" and then give them what they had a right to and keep the rest to yourself. That would require some smart thinking but at least it wouldn't be a lie. This skill could have made me a lawyer. In fact, someone said to me, "When you grow up you're going to be a preacher or a lying lawyer." At any rate, I now had a way of getting off the hook without committing a sin.

Jesus cured the blind and the lame. That impressed me. Then I wondered why He just cured a few of them. Why didn't He cure all of them or teach other people how to do it? But raising the dead to life was too much for me. Lazarus, who was already decaying in the grave, was raised from the dead, and then he had to die all over again later. That didn't seem like a favor to me—dying once was bad enough!!

Jesus also walked on water, multiplied loaves of bread, and changed water into wine. Now those were miracles I could warm up to. But I didn't see any point to other stories they told us.

There was the story about St. Januarius whose dried up blood was kept in a vial in a Church in Naples (he died a martyr). Each year on his feast day the priest would bring the vial of dried up blood out on the balcony of the Church and hold it up, turn it back and forth and the blood would liquefy. The crowd would go wild. I never got the lesson here! Unless it was that God could do that. Why *that*, when so many other things needed to be done?

Fatima and the visionaries really put some fear into me. The Blessed Mother had warned these kids about disaster and suffering to come if the world did not repent. A statue of Our Lady of Fatima was brought around from one town to another. It was so beautiful and realistic. It was carried in procession and enthroned amidst candles and flowers. The whole church smelled like incense. The night she came to our Church it poured down rain like there would be a flood. Someone told me that was a "sign" from Our Lady. She liked rain and it usually rained when she arrived. I thought, *I had better get serious and clean up my act.*

16

The Blessed Mother really had an effect on the weather. One time at Fatima thousands of people were soaking wet in the pouring rain. All of a sudden the sun came out and began to wobble around, and then headed straight for the earth. Then it was back in the sky and all the people were perfectly dry. That was really enough to make me wet!

The Sisters always wore black and white. They had a lot of starched linen around their faces and a big white shield-like piece of starched linen that came down from their neck almost to their waist. Their clothes fascinated me. They wore these large black rosary beads on their belts, that hung down to the floor. That was a blessing as you could always hear them coming! Some of the Sisters had learned to ball their rosary beads up in their hand when they were sneaking up on a kid.

Many of the nuns were very young and a few of them were very pretty. One day I was looking at one of the pretty ones and wondered if she had boobs under that starched white thing! *Oh, God forgive me!* I knew that was a "mortal" but how could I tell the priest?

One thing I did know was that they had all kinds of objects stored underneath that stiff white collar. They were always reaching up under there and pulling out a tiny watch, paper clips, a pen, needles, Band Aids or scissors. I thought they must have a small china press under there at least.

We were delighted when we saw a lock of a Sister's hair sticking out from under her bonnet. Then it became a game to find out what color hair each Sister had.

I asked Sister if Jesus was God, she said, "Yes, Jesus is God."

I said, "But I thought God was invisible and Jesus is a man. How can they be the same?"

Then she explained about three persons in one God which, she reminded me, I should have learned that in Catechism in the second grade. I could not see how three people could be one. Sister held up a paper three-leaf clover and explained, "this is a clover and it has three leaves but all three are one." I figured *God has three parts* and asked no more questions, as I had had a hard time with numbers all through school. Besides, further questions would have led to "take it on faith!"

The boys were almost as tall as one Sister and some of the girls were even taller. We told her that her name was too long for such a short nun. Then she wrote, "Sister Mary Athanasius Smith" on the blackboard and under it she wrote the name of a short boy, "James Patrick Clark, Junior" and said, "His name is longer than mine." I don't know what we learned from that except that she was a human being just like we were, despite the strange clothes she wore. We often visited Sister Athanasius on the recess ground. She always had cookies in her big wide sleeve and was ready to talk with us.

A smart-aleck Sister with a square face and some hairs growing out of her chin used to say sarcastic things that she thought were funny but we didn't. She called one kid "Fatty Felix" all the time. His name was Jim. The poor fellow was traumatized every time the class laughed at the name, "Fatty Felix." (I'm sure he discussed this with his analyst years later.) The smart-alecky Sister also used to assign readings that were not in the book. It didn't matter because the next day she had forgotten what she had done and never asked us about it. Fifth grade was a complete wash-out!

Some kids used to sneak out and climb up the bell tower over the Cathedral. They could have killed themselves. I never could figure out why the kids weren't afraid they might slip on pigeon crap which was all over the ladder going up the bell tower. Most of them never got caught but our Principal with her big black eyes and a turned-down mouth got wind of what was going on, and there was a general assembly, at which she ranted and raved, demanding that anyone who had climbed up the bell tower should raise his or her hand and confess their crime. Two boys finally raised their hands.

Sister had the big ruler up her sleeve. The two seventh-grade boys walked up and one at a time they "got the big ruler." It was a terrifying sight, sort of like an execution. The hand was extended palm up and Sister made a terrible face as she raised the ruler in the air and came down with a swish and we heard a *pop.* I thought the kid's hand would fall off. It took about five minutes to complete this scene of horror. We left the assembly hall in silence, no one looking at any one, we were frozen with fear.

The two boys were the center of attention after school that day. They were very cool, saying, "Naw, it didn't hurt." "I think she enjoyed it," "She's a born sadist." "She got her jollies."

One Sister turned me on to reading. She gave me a book called, "Freddie and the Ignormus." It was a whimsical story but I devoured it. Then there were sequels. From then on I would go to the Public Library and get five or six books at a time, with a note from Sister saying it was OK. When the inevitable "overdue" bill came my mother flipped out!

Then one day I didn't have my homework and Sister told me to take my books and go out in the hall and not come back in that class until I had finished my homework. I had to sit on the floor in the hallway to do the work. It was most uncomfortable. Kids kept passing by and teasing me, so I decided to get up and go home where I could work in peace. I could come back to class the next day and turn in my homework.

The next day I proudly appeared at the desk with my homework. Sister said nothing and pointed to the desk for me to lay it down. Nothing was said until two o'clock and that was dismissal time. Sister said in a cold voice, "William, stand up!"

I stood up.

She went into a rampage about my leaving school without permission. Her tirade went on for about fifteen minutes. When we finally got out of there the kids almost killed me for making them late. I was doing exactly what she told me to do, don't come back in the classroom until you have finished your homework.

Sister Principal had a clicker which she used in church.

We walked in a straight line; one head directly in line with the one in front of you. When we walked in church she would click it for us to genuflect all together, click it again for all to turn and go in the pew, and click it again for all to sit. One kid had learned to make a sound with his mouth that sounded exactly like her clicker and used to do it on the recess ground. We dared him to do it in Church. Then unexpectedly when we all genuflected at the click, turned to go in the pew, and sat down at the click, we heard another click and we all stood up. Sister ran down the aisle like a quarterback to the front of the Church. Her face was blood red against her white starch. She yelled, "Sit down!" We all sat down. She demanded to know who did that. No one admitted doing it and no other clicker was ever found.

One morning when I had missed Mass, I thought I would study my spelling words while other kids went to the cafeteria to eat breakfast. The Sister asked me how to spell "abstract."

I had not studied yet, so I said, "I don't know how."

Sister said, "It is on the list for today!"

I didn't think any more about it. When all the kids came back to the classroom Sister told four of us to go to the board and write the words she called out. "Abstract!" was one of the first words she called out. I got them all correct. When we sat down she said, "William, how is it that you could not spell abstract when you came to school a few minutes ago, but just now you spelled it perfectly on the board?"

I said, "Because I studied it." Then I realized she was accusing me of cheating and my face turned red. She took this as a sure sign that I was cheating and said so! From then on anytime there was a question about who lied or stole something, my face turned red. I wondered if there was any cure for blushing.

On another occasion we had to line up against the wall

21

The Serpent before the fall –
When he could talk and walk...

Eve before the fall – no clothes on.....

and take off our shoes and socks, and take everything out of our pockets because someone had stolen some money off Sister's desk. I'm sure my face was blood red. If it was not in anyone's socks or pockets, there was only one other place it could be on a kid and I prayed there wouldn't be a strip search.

When we were going to the weekly confession box, the priest in the confessional yelled out loud to me, "How old are you?" I did not know whether to push my age up or push it down. The kids asked me "Why did he yell at you?"

I said, "Who knows!" Maybe he was having a bad day.

The stories in the Bible were still bothering me. The story about God creating everything in seven days was cool! I liked that. I didn't know anything about science then, but even so, the story about Adam and Eve and the Serpent raised questions in my mind. They said the Serpent was punished by being made to crawl on his belly! How did he get around before that? It also occurred to me that snakes don't talk. But the story of Cain and Abel sounded realistic. One brother is the pet and one brother is bad. One night I was trying to count my ribs and my mother said, "Don't be silly!" I did not discuss the story about Adam's rib with her for fear she would contradict the Bible.

God turning Lot's wife into a pillar of salt because she looked back at the burning cities seemed awfully cruel. A man being struck dead because he touched the Sacred Ark of the Covenant, trying to steady it, was another cruel stroke. When the bears ate the little boys for laughing of Elijah I thought, *God is awful touchy. You better be careful!*

The Ten Commandments seemed reasonable to me. Ten is not too many rules, not near as many as we had in Catholic School! Besides I was in no danger of breaking most of them. Especially the one about adultery since I was not married. But according to the Sister a lot of other things fell under that commandment and were serious sins. I didn't think playing with yourself belonged there. (Of course, I didn't bring that up in class.)

One Sister always told stories about good kids who committed a mortal sin and then died suddenly. At the end of the story she would always say, "Little did he know that he would die that night." We used to call her "Sister Littledidheknow." I wondered if these kids died right after playing with themselves? I had heard it could cause you to go blind but I never heard that it could *kill* you! So I brushed that thought away.

There was a story about a little boy who always slept with his hands under the covers at night. One night a raving wolf came up the steps to his bedroom and jumped on top of

23

him. The boy couldn't get his hands out from under the covers to make the sign of the cross so he yelled out "Jesus, Mary and Joseph!" The snarling wolf fell off the bed, rolled down the stairs and out the front door (we all knew that the wolf was the devil). I had heard my father say "Jesus, Mary and Joseph!" when he was exasperated about something but he wasn't praying. The lesson of the story was "always sleep with your hands above the covers." I thought, *Why is that, since yelling out a prayer works just as well?* I couldn't take that advice seriously! Despite all this, the weight was on God's side and Sister was right there with Him. So now, I prayed for forgiveness for my doubts. When I heard about doubting Thomas I felt relieved. I liked him!

My math grades were dismal, although I did well in everything else. At the end of eighth grade Sister told me that I had failed math and could not go on to High School.

"I'll just do eighth grade over again," I said, hoping to placate her.

She looked at me, saying. "Aren't you upset about it?"

I replied, "No, it's OK."

Apparently that was the right answer because she passed me and I went on the High School. If I had cried, she might have held me back.

One Sister was really nice on the recess ground. The boys would gather around her and talk with her. She seemed to understand us and she would laugh with us. It was like she had been a boy before she turned into a nun. She was a decent ball player too! We told her the stories that came from Sister "Littledidheknow." She would crack up laughing.

One day she said, "You know, boys, I'll see you after school out by the see-saws. I know what you are talking about."

We glanced at each other because we knew what we

"Sister Littledidheknow"

Sister Babe Ruth!

were talking about too! How did she know? Sister said, "You are probably talking about sex. And you are probably getting it all mixed up. If you want to know the facts you need to find out from your parents, or ask the priest to talk to you about it when he comes around for instructions."

At our next meeting at the see-saws we all agreed not to talk to our parents or the priest; we knew they wouldn't tell us the nitty gritty. So we kept on sharing bits of information, looking up words in the dictionary, and showing each other the *National Geographic* and *Sunshine and Health* magazines. (Those two magazines were the only ones where you saw people without clothes on.)

That dear Sister wanted us to get some realistic sex instructions, but of course it would have been unthinkable in those days. I don't know if Sister had ever heard of wet dreams—but we had! I used to worry that wet dreams might come under the sixth commandment since so much stuff came under that heading.

The Sister who talked and laughed with us on the playground said in class, "Boys and girls, you are growing up now. You should always be neat and clean. Take a bath every night and always smell good." The next day the whole room smelled of talcum powder, Chanel #5, and Hi Karti! This beloved Sister started laughing out loud saying, "I only meant soap and water." I thought of my Irish father's saying, "If you can't come clean, come smelling good!"

In our eighth grade graduation picture the boys were kneeling down. Each one was wearing a two-tone "leisure jacket!" (thank God they don't make them anymore). The girls loomed like Amazons in back of us with white dresses and some God-awful thing in their hair that made them look foolish. Sister Principal stood regally on the end, with clicker in hand and the skinny Monsignor stood on the other end looking sad. It was a funky picture.

II

Growing Up in High School

Bishop Murphy High School was the boys' destination, and Little Flower High School was the girls' destination. Catholic schools always separated the boys from the girls in High School. I guessed that was sort of silent sex education, and that taught us something basic right away.

The high school I attended had 500 boys and a six-foot, six-inch priest in a long black cassock who was in charge, along with eight other priests, with a Sister for math and a Sister librarian.

This was a different environment altogether. We each had a locker to put our stuff in. You could talk in the hallways, you didn't have to walk in a straight line, and you changed rooms for each class.

It was like a breath of fresh air! Until the seniors started throwing us down the stairs, chopping off our hair when they caught us outside of school, and making us wear stupid beanies.

During Freshman Economics Class, the priest one day yelled, "Some one farted in here, open the window!" Now I had never heard a nun talk like that. What a shock! He could have said, "broke wind" or "unfragrant flatulence" or something nicer but maybe he came from the same part of Ireland as my father.

The school was an old building and each room had an opening that used to be a fireplace. One day a boy brought a

28

cat to school and put it inside the fireplace opening and covered the opening with something. During class the cat would go "meow." The priest thought it was one of the boys and demanded to know who was making that noise. About that time, the cat got loose and walked up to the front of the room. The priest grabbed it and threw it out of the window.

In the Biology Lab there was a cat preserved in a jar. The cat had been there through several generations of students, but we started the rumor that it was the cat the priest threw out the window. Any respectable cat would have survived that toss out the first floor window.

The most often asked question in religion class was "Is it a sin to tongue kiss a girl?" The priest would say, "It is not a sin in itself but it is a near occasion of sin, so you should not do it." This time I agreed heartily with church teaching; that was a nasty thing to do!

We had Confession once a month. Each priest would sit in his classroom in a chair and one at a time we would go in, kneel down and tell our sins. There was one priest who al-

29

After nine lives and one priest...

ways put his face in his hands while hearing Confession. When you finished he would mumble, "Say three Hail Marys," and mumble absolution. That was a breeze. We all knew to go to that priest; he gave you absolution with no questions and no lecture no matter what you confessed. He always had a long, long line outside his door.

Another priest was extremely pious and would give you five minutes or so of spiritual direction and advice. He never had more than two or three customers waiting for his services, whom we called "the Seminarians."

One day I got the pious priest. After confessing the terrible "M" word, he said, "Son, when you have thoughts that occasion this sin, try to think about something else, like baseball."

I thought to myself, *That's not nearly as interesting as what I was thinking about.*

Then he said, "This sin is just a habit. We are creatures of habit. When the twig is bent one way, you have to bend it the other way with constant effort." I thought, *My twig will stand straight up no matter which way I bend it.*

The six-foot, six-inch Principal challenged us in religion class about our faith. He said, "How do you know all of the things you are being taught are true? How do you know there is a God? How do you know that Jesus ever existed?"

He gave us a few days to think about it. Then he asked again, "How do you know there is a God?" Most of us had not really given it much thought but we fumbled around trying to think of an answer that would suit him, *knowing that he was about to tell us the answer.*

Everything had a cause. If everything was caused by something in the past and you traced the causes back, it surely could not go on forever. There would have to be a "First Cause" that caused everything that exists, and which holds all things in existence.

We all agreed that that made perfect sense. I wavered because I thought, *Matter is neither created nor destroyed and some things happen by chance.* I dared not say this to the six-foot-six-inch principal. One very bright boy who stuttered raised his hand and said, "F-f-father those proofs don't h-h-hold w-w-water."

The priest walked down the aisle and towered over him saying, "Are you smarter than Thomas Aquinas?"

"N-n-no, F-f-Father."

We got the entire scoop about how Jesus ordained the twelve Apostles with Peter as their leader and the unbroken chain of successors down to the present Pope. Then about

31

Martin Luther taking things into his own hands with no authority to do so. I accepted without question that this was an accurate account of history. This must be the true Church!

Then when I heard that outside the church (meaning outside the Catholic Church), there is no salvation, I rebelled. *Most of the world was not Catholic. Most of my friends were not Catholic. I couldn't believe that they were all going to Hell!* I heard that statement only one time. It was never mentioned again.

Dad would call the Monsignor, "big-ass Pete," and make fun of church stuff. Mother would try to make him go to Confession and Communion once a year, but he refused. My mother said, "Pat, we can't bury you in the church if you don't make your Easter duty."

His response, "Well that's your problem! I won't be there." I used to pray for my Dad all the time. I was worried about his salvation.

My mother had just hung a large picture of the Sacred Heart of Jesus in the dining room. I was lying on the floor doing homework. I looked up and saw my father staring at the picture for a long time. I thought, *He is finally getting religion!*

I said, "Dad, what are you thinking?"

He said, "Jesus wasn't a bad-looking man, was he," and then continued reading the newspaper. My heart sank. He was a good man, just not interested in church—especially not in Confession.

Sister John of the Cross, the math teacher, used to hit a kid named Elmore over the head with a book every now and then, we never knew why. He was a shy little guy who sat in the first desk, first row. Clear out of the blue, Sister would rush over and hit him over the head. No one ever figured out why—nor did poor Elmore. Now and then she had a sudden spasm, and would head for Elmore!

She forgot her meds!!

Now the priests were putting the bug on me to become a priest. I noticed that they all seemed to drive good-looking new cars. Some of them smoked; I guess that's why there was no prohibition against smoking on the recess ground. I took a message over to the priests' house late one afternoon and a priest answered the door with a beer in his hand. That looked like a pretty easy life to me.

I was so convinced of my religion, despite doubts and guilt that I started talking about being a monk so I could get to Heaven. The kids said, "You couldn't keep quiet for five minutes." I set out to prove that I could. The kids gathered around me and started saying stupid things. Finally, I cracked up laughing, couldn't help it.

They started yelling, "You broke silence! We knew you couldn't keep quiet for five minutes."

Chaperones – preventing sin! ! !

(sure cure for concupiscence)

I said, "I will when I'm living with monks and not monkeys!"

The priests made fun of me about the monk thing. Dad angrily said I was crazy. I finally had gotten his attention. This was the first time he had spoken to me directly since childhood. . . .

Teen Town and the Prom were always heavily supervised by older ladies who sat in a line on a bench, watching every move we made. There was no close dancing and no going outside. I guess they thought we were about to commit a sin as soon as we were out of their sight. My main exposure to girls was going to St. Agatha's Girls' School to be in stage plays. It was a boarding school run by Sisters. One play had a boy about to kiss a girl when a ringing phone would stop the action. Opening night, the girl in charge of stage props couldn't find the alarm clock to be used for the phone ring. The boy paused and then gave the girl a long passionate kiss. The Sisters were almost hysterical. It was like one of their girls had lost her innocence!

One practice night Sister threatened to lock me in a closet if I didn't go on home after play practice. To get her off my back, I confided to her that I was going to be a monk. She said, "Get going."

III

Growing Up in the Seminary

Education gets more profound in the Seminary, which teaches you how to think logically; that means in "syllogisms." Don't look the word up, I'm going to tell you what it means. You start with a statement such as "all trees are green," That is called a major premise. Then you add a second statement, such as "This is a tree," which is a minor premise. The conclusion will be "this is green." Ingenious! If you follow this formula you will infallibly get the right answer. The catch here is that your major premise must be true or you'll get a wrong conclusion.

Relax, that's as far as I'm going with this! You know enough to get through life without syllogisms, I'm sure. But apparently seminarians didn't.

Philosophy taught us the ideas of Plato and Aristotle, and then other philosophers down to Wittgenstein and the post-modernists. It pointed out where each great thinker went wrong throughout history. I really liked some of those wrong thinkers like Nietzsche and Schopenhauer. I read them privately until someone told me they were on the "Index of Forbidden Books." I was told that we could only read "Christian Existentialists." The sin had already been committed.

It seemed Plato and Aristotle were the only ones who got it right. Then Thomas Aquinas really got the answers! He leaned on Aristotle for a lot of this. I thought the Domini-

Sesquipedalian Words!

cans were smart because Thomas Aquinas was one of them. That is, until the Jesuits showed up in the books contradicting them on a number of points. I liked that! Jesuits to the rescue again!

Dogmatic Theology took each infallible statement of the Church and proved it to be true by Scripture and Tradition. It also pointed out how all the great religious thinkers throughout the ages were either heretics or gone astray. Imagine that! It took each individual dogma of the Church and classified it as: "infallible," "close to infallible," and "beliefs commonly held and it would be offensive to pious ears to deny them." How can you tell the difference between "pious ears and regular ears?" We learned how the Last Supper gradually developed into the formal Eucharist. In the early days different countries had different ways of celebrating. One interesting thing was how the "Canon" developed. Originally the presider prayed spontaneously and read the Scriptures, then said the Prayer of Consecration, followed by sharing the consecrated bread and wine.

Sometimes the presider got carried away, and it lasted for hours. Finally, the Church decided that the essential prayers should be said according to a formula called the "Canon of the Mass," thus squelching the long winded.

Moral Theology explained what was right and what was sinful in every realm of human behavior. It left nothing to your common sense. It explained minutely how to determine if an act was seriously sinful. It was insulting to your intelligence. However, it was pretty good when treating the sixth commandment. Some interesting situations came up there!! Some things which I had never thought of. And we were allowed to think about them deliberately! The professor said, "But don't entertain these thoughts." We tried not to but the thoughts kept entertaining us. (See X-rated section.)

The Scripture Professor was an engaging personality with enormous knowledge. At that time (late fifties), "literary historical criticism" was allowed to be taught in Catholic Seminaries. It had been used for years among Protestant scholars. The Bible was approached as literature. The historical context of each book was explored. This was an eye-opener to me. All my favorite Scripture quotes turned out not to mean what I thought they meant! Knowing the historical context gave new meaning to the words. That brought my faith to life! The development of Revelation was formed in historical events. It was put in writing by many different authors. Inspiration did not mean that the Holy Spirit dictated each word. It was told in the human language of the times. The authors used drama, poetry and history, as they understood it, to proclaim God's message. The Holy Spirit used human instruments to do the work. Now religion was making real sense to me!

I was very disturbed to find out that the first twelve chapters of Genesis were pre-history. They were folklore about the beliefs of the Jewish people! Does that mean the Adam and Eve story is not factual? Yes, it meant it was a story about our relationship to God.

I was appalled and resisted mightily! Quasi-history mixed with folklore begins with Abraham. Even Kings I and II are still filled with political spin, luscious tales, and religious tradition.

I felt I was losing my faith. *All* scholars were saying these things which I thought were dangerous. Maybe the scholars were all Communists out to undermine the faith! It was the fifties, the McCarthy era.

Church History class was like a long epic drama. Shocking, exhilarating, discouraging—but real. Real life, real people, God's people, good and bad.

Pope Alexander VI turned the crucifix toward the wall while he drank and played poker with his friends; his illegitimate children and his total decadence are examples of facts which shocked. My faith was wavering!

Then came the history of the Councils of the Church, the first of which, Chalcedon, was convened by the Emperor, not the Pope, and the bloody battles in the streets and the fights among the Bishops that preceded the Council.

This was shaking my naïve ideas that the Apostles put on vestments and started saying Mass, and Peter put on the Tiara and was Pope right from the beginning. I was either going to grow up and face facts or lose my faith. A student said to the professor one day, "When does it get better?" (See end note #1, Page 78.)

Believe it or not, future priests had classes in how to

preach well, called homiletics. My professor said, "Have a good beginning, a good ending and put them close together" and, "the mind can only absorb as much as the rear end can endure." He also said, "It takes at least an hour to prepare a five-minute homily. It takes five minutes to prepare a one-hour homily!"

I slept through Canon Law class, so I can't describe it!

When time came for ordination, we were required to take the oath against modernism. By the late fifties we had been pretty well educated in literary historical criticism and some other things called "errors" in this document. Pope Pius XII wrote an Encyclical approving the use of literary historical criticism. So I took the oath without any question but with some confusion.

There was a post-ordination year of Pastoral Theology which taught us how to administer the sacraments and serve the faithful. This consisted of listening to the professor talk about his colorful years in the Ministry! Ugh!

It also consisted of more interesting events like practicing how to say Mass and administer the sacraments. We practiced saying Mass with a professor observing. I got a note saying I had made over fifty mistakes during my final practice. I told this to my elderly confessor because I was worried. He said, "Do you know how to say the words of consecration?"

I said, "Yes."

He replied, "Then don't worry about the rest." Thank God!

I was scandalized when I heard one seminarian singing "This Magic Moment" right before his friend practiced the words of consecration!

Theology was in Latin. Along the way we also had courses in Hebrew and Greek. These languages were supposed to help us read the Original Scriptures, which none of us ever did as far as I know. I kept the Greek New Testament bent open, so that when they asked me to read Greek on my orals, it would fall open to a passage I had rehearsed.

My Catholic education kept me out of a lot of trouble! It gave me a delicate conscience. It gave me a fine scholastic foundation. The negative side of my education is that it left me feeling that I was never good enough and with feelings of guilt beyond belief.

IV
Growing Up in Ministry

I come no longer to make you laugh: Things now,
That bear weighty and serious brow;
Sad high and full of dignity and woe;
Noble scenes that draw the eyes to flow,
We now present.

William Shakespeare
Henry VIII

What was life like as a priest? My first assignment was in the Missions of Appalachia. Two priests took care of seven churches scattered throughout the mountains along with a maximum security prison.

At a Conference at the Headquarters of the Diocese, the Bishop asked, "Bill where are you stationed now?"

"In Appalachia," I said. He just rolled his eyes and looked to Heaven. That assignment was like Siberia to most priests.

These mountain people were simple, kind, and loving. If they liked you, you could do no wrong. If they didn't like you, you better leave town. They never complained when we were late, they just sat and visited and greeted us with smiles when we arrived. We were privileged to share their joys and their heartbreaks and their meals, including squirrel on one or two occasions which brought tears to my eyes!

Two women in one small church never spoke to each

other. Being young and fervent I got them together for a talk.

"You both are fine ladies. You come up to Holy Communion side by side to receive Our Lord. That means you are united in Him. It is not right for you not to speak to each other."

They both left with heads down absolutely silent, not saying a word. From that day on neither of them ever spoke to me again.

One small Church was Polish. All the men sat on one side and all of the women sat on the other side. When they went to Confession, they rattled off their sins in Polish. It sounded terrible but I knew it couldn't be so bad since most of them were elderly people! I gave them absolution without a clue as to what they had said!

Mourning (in Polish)

At Mass they would bring up home-churned butter, milk, and eggs in the Offertory procession. When there was a funeral, the deceased was laid out at home in the living room. The Mass *had* to be in Latin (long after English was the norm). The coffin was loaded on a truck and the pallbearers jumped on. After the burial, all the women would go around visiting the graves of people, long since deceased, weeping and moaning the whole time. The only Polish I ever learned was how to pronounce their names, and "*Jak się masz* (good morning) *and dzięń* dobry (good day)."

In a small coal-mining town there was a mean guy who would terrorize the people, so everybody stayed out of his way. He was shot and killed. I asked if the man who killed him was arrested. They said, "Naw; he needed killing!" the local police agreed with them.

Another coal-mining town had a large contingent of Italian immigrants. Charlie Busini told me that when he came to the U.S.A. as a young man, he expected to pick up dollar bills on the streets of this rich country. After forty years, of working in the coal mines, he never made enough money to go back home to Italy.

Every week I took Holy Communion, early in the morning, to an elderly lady named Rosario. She was very talkative. I always noticed a pungent odor, it smelled like raw potatoes. I asked one of her friends what that smell was. She laughed and said, "That was vodka, Father. Why do you think she talks so much?"

There was pettiness and bickering especially at Parish Council Meetings. One time a little group of ladies wanted to buy "beauty parlor pink" carpet for the Sanctuary of the Church.

I said, "We can't do that, it is not appropriate."

I wanted to say, "That color belongs in a brothel," but I was afraid they would say, "How do you know?"

From then on these ladies hated me. That was a learning experience. I had never encountered such animosity before, but this adversity was good for me!! "Love those who hate you!"

In my naiveté, I had a lot of illusions, and even prejudices. Working with such a variety of people broadened my perspective and it was easier to love them.

My next assignment was to an upscale Parish closer to a big city. The rectory was brand new, and the people were more sophisticated. New learning experience for me!

One middle-aged gentleman came to me in tears one day, and said, "I'm depressed and can't go on; I have not received Holy Communion in twenty years!" (I had noticed that at Mass.) "I am a homosexual, rejected and despised."

I said, "Do you have a family?"

He continued, "I had a wonderful mother who became an invalid. I cared for her until she died."

I said, "Brothers or sisters?"

"Yes, three brothers and two sisters. We were very poor but I had a good job so I put them all through college. Now they are scattered around the country."

"Did you go to college? I asked.

"No, I never had the time. I had to work to support them all. Now, I'm too old."

I said, "I'm going to give you absolution. For your penance, thank God for His grace, and continue living the generous, caring life that you have lived in the past, and be faithful to your partner. You are always welcome in this Church. We respect you and love you."

I knew homosexuals were often viewed as evil people because Scripture condemns their actions. (Scripture also condemns divorce and re-marriage, promiscuous behavior, lying, cheating, stealing—but sinners come to Christ in Holy Communion because He welcomes sinners!)

In the Seminary, we were taught to treat homosexuals with compassion and to encourage them to be good Christians, never refusing them absolution.

My sister the nun spent the night at my rectory on her way home from somewhere. She was in full habit. The next day it was all over town that the priest had a nun stay overnight with him.

They didn't know that she took off her veil and rosary beads, kicked off her shoes and had a whiskey sour.

Another time the rumor got around that I had a "girlfriend." I had heard this several times. One Sunday at the end of Mass I said, "I want to thank you for a great compliment! Some of you have said that I have a 'girlfriend.' Thanks for thinking that I am still young enough and attractive enough to have such luck. Unfortunately—it's not true."

Next, I was stationed in a small town as a university

chaplain. University life was good. We had good music led by a Mormon; the lead guitar was a Baptist, and the congregation was made up of young and old from all over the town. Those three years were fun.

There was one glitch. The Bishop had sent me there without telling me that I would have to get rid of the Episcopal and Presbyterian Ministers who were sharing office space in the Catholic Center. The two chaplains were doing abortion counseling with students, so they had to go!

This was an agony for me. In telling them of the decision, one of them countered, "I wish you were more of an S.O.B., so I could hate you!" Neither I, nor the Diocese, had investigated whether or not they were actually *recommending* abortion!

The students were discussing abortion one night and they were saying that a woman who has an abortion commits murder. I said, "I don't think women have abortions casually. My impression is that they are often under severe emotional stress of some kind."

A student said, "That doesn't excuse the murder."

A few days later, one young lady came to the Catholic Center asking for some counseling. She said she had been at the meeting and was in tears. Here was her story. She had been married to a young man and they had three children in rapid succession. The husband refused to *practice birth control because he was Catholic.* One day he walked out on her and the kids and never came back. She could never contact him. She had no means of support. She was in nursing school at the University for three or four years while raising three children. During that time she was seeing a young man and she became pregnant. It would be impossible to have another child, as she had no family and no money. She panicked and had an abortion.

She had been miserable since that day. I consoled her,

Monsignor backing up to go home. . .

gave her absolution and assured her that God loved her. After she left I was sad for awhile. Then I remembered that abortion was a "reserved sin." I was supposed to get permission from the Bishop to absolve her from it! Nevertheless the absolution was valid!! God's Mercy had been dispensed without permission. (See end note #2, Page 78.)

One morning the Chancellor of the Diocese called me to inquire about my being arrested for drunk driving. I said, "No, Monsignor, that was Monsignor Bolin. I am Father Nolan." The names must have sounded alike. The offender's name had appeared in the newspaper and was announced on TV as well. Maybe he called me because I was the younger man and only a priest.

The real story was that Monsignor Bolin had been out to dinner in town, and had had a few drinks too many. On the way home he was pulled over by the police because he was weaving between the lanes. The two policemen, who were devout Catholics, saw that the offender was "the Monsignor," so they said, "Monsignor, we saw you crossing the yellow line slightly, so we will follow you home to make sure you get there safely."

They got in their police car which was in back of "Monsignor's" car. The "Monsignor" got in his brand new Cadillac and instead of putting it in drive, he put it in reverse, stepped on the gas and slammed into the front of the police car! The two policemen had no choice but to take him in because now they had a wrecked police car to explain. The lesson to be learned here is: always be sure your gear shift is on 'D for drive' if you want to go forward.

One night during a study group, a student arrived late and said, "Father, who is that kid sitting on the back steps smoking a joint?" It was my sixteen-year-old nephew who was visiting me. After my tirade, my nephew informed me that I was "out of contact" with reality. I said, "Well, where are you when you are stoned?" He left the next day.

As a priest you share precious moments and tragic moments with people who are just like you: They are your family! Some of them get on your nerves, some of them drive you nuts, some are considerate and kind, some are indifferent to you, some don't like you, but they are *all* your family and they put up with your foibles also.

V

Growing as a Priest

Priests can "unwind" with each other. It is a professional fellowship. This association with priests taught me about their humanness, their struggles and their complaints, which were very similar to my own. One recurring topic after sports and jokes was the Bishop. The commentary was usually negative. On the rare occasion when the Bishop was present he was given accolades. After all, he was the boss! He could give and take away parishes! Bishops had a club of their own, consisting of Bishops only. We had no idea what they talked about when they got together! More about Bishops later.

Priests are a motley group. They are rugged individuals; sometimes loners and always stars. I was attracted to the humorous ones.

From the very beginning there was a divide between the conservatives and the liberals. After Vatican II, the rift widened. If you were all for the changes, you were to the left, perhaps dangerous. If you wanted everything to stay as it was, you were safe, to be trusted.

Most of my parishioners were wary of changes—meaning they hated it! They would harass the local priests as if it was our entire fault.

My pastor took down the communion rail and used it as part of the back drop for the new free standing altar. All hell broke loose. At Sunday Mass he said, "Some of our

Protestant neighbors think we worship the statues. I'm beginning to think some of you worshiped the altar rail."

Going from Latin to English was a major crisis. The same pastor said, "Latin is the universal language, universally not understood all over the world."

Post Vatican II was a rough time for priests because the parishioners all wanted you to agree with them!

At a priest conference when some of the older priests were complaining about Vatican II, one of them stood up and said, "What do you young priests want?" A young priest stood up and said, "We just want all of us to be aware of what is going on today." The fighting among the clergy and among the people was not encouraging!

If you were enthusiastic for Vatican II, you were a raving liberal, or a hippie. Priests were leaving to get married every day!

One older priest said to me, "When are you leaving?" Every time he saw me, he said, "Are you still with us?"

Here is a terrible example of how acrimonious things got. A healthy handsome twenty-eight year old priest had an allergic reaction to the anesthesia during an appendectomy and died. His liturgies were innovative and upbeat. He was full of love for everyone and expressed it freely.

A few weeks after his funeral an elderly nun said to me, "Thank goodness we are free of him!" I lost it and told her off, but I was aware of how much her whole community disapproved of that priest. If you were liberal, you were "bad." If you were conservative, you were "good."

There was no balance in public disputes; no real dialogue or respect shown to fellow Catholics. It was a terrible time to be a priest but most of us had great hope for a new day in the Church because of John XXIII!

After a while things quieted down. The "hootenanny Masses" and the "awful guitar Masses" faded. The music

The People of God – The Church

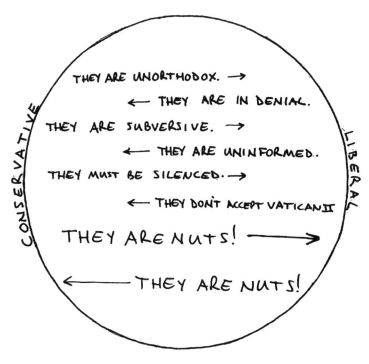

Every family has its little problems.

was better; in fact some of the new music like "On Eagle Wings" and "Here I Am, Lord" became popular even with the most "orthodox."

From 1979 or 1980, there started a trend to "undo" Vatican II. That trend has endured until today.

Arch-conservatives accused hard working priests of being unorthodox and not loyal to the present Pope or even to Catholicism. Some priests call these reactionaries fanatics! Bad stuff!!!

Then came the horrible pedophilia scandal of 2000. A retreat priest in <u>1983,</u> told all our priests it was coming. There had been articles about it but <u>nothing</u> was done. The Bishops tried to cover it up. They hid behind their lawyers. They were more concerned with avoiding lawsuits than with telling the truth. Families and victims were devastated. Faith in our leadership diminished but Catholics kept on believing and supporting the Church. This was a doomsday event—still not recognized as such by our leaders!

Jesus came to cast fire on the earth—the consuming fire of compassion for <u>all human beings.</u> Where is His fire in the Catholic Church today? Catholics seem to be defending their positions as the only truth and condemning everyone who doesn't agree with <u>them.</u> That's a simplistic statement but it seems to be true.

Where do Bishops come from? They are made by "asexual reproduction" as one priest said. Here's how it works. Bishops send to Rome names of priests that they think would make good Bishops. The names are of priests whom the Bishops have been close to in some way, priests who worked in the Head Office or supported the Bishop, and who were willing to "suck up" to some extent. It's no wonder Bishops resemble each other. It's sort of an incestuous family!

You could say good qualifications for a Bishop candidate are:

1. Roman education
2. Job at headquarters
3. Degree in Canon Law
4. Good administrator
5. Good fund raiser
6. Knows how to speak Italian
7. Can read Latin
8. Clean record
9. Neat appearance (Looks and charm help a lot)
10. Sound theology
11. Devotion to the Pope
12. Not a "loose canon," i.e.; careful how he expresses himself in public.

In the Early Church, Bishops were chosen by the local people who knew them well. That was too messy, and as the Church became more centralized in Imperial Rome, the present system was devised, in order to give greater control to headquarters.

The Administrative Church operates like a business. The CEO of the local franchise is called a Bishop. The Bishop is over all the salesmen priests. All salesmen forego marriage in order to serve the company better. The Bishop owns all the property and all the assets of the Diocese. (This was arranged because of an historical incident when lay trustees took over ownership and management of church property and assets.)

The customers are the lay people who donate for the services received, and offer volunteer services.

Cardinals are the Arch-Bishops of the largest and richest cities throughout the world. The Chief Executive of the whole conglomerate is the Pope. Each of the centers has a full staff of accountants, fund raisers, planners, secretaries and lawyers. The Pope has a whole city for his staff including a post office, a train station, and a small army with spears.

Local Headquarters lends money to customers to build churches and schools. When the customers finally pay off the bill, at six percent interest, the buildings belong to the Bishop. They are deeded in his name. The customers are aware of the deal, so it's not illegal. Slick business! Better still! The Company *does not pay income taxes.* This vast conglomerate runs smoothly.

There are problem areas. Some customers are living in second marriages that have not been approved by the wise Judges of the Tribunal (yes, the System has a legal court and Canon lawyers). (See X-rated section.)

Some customers are practicing "artificial birth control" instead of "natural birth control." They may be broke, out of work or worn out and feel they can't have more children, but they are violating "natural law." (See end note #3, Page 80.)

Some customers are homosexual. It is not a sin to *be* a homosexual. No one knows why you are one. (It might be genetic or early conditioning so it is not your fault.) Sexual acts between people of the same sex are forbidden by Scripture and the "natural law." The Pope publicly disapproved of marriage between gays. (See X-rated section.)

Church leaders know that a significant number of salesmen priests are homosexual. Who do you think designed all those lovely vestments and choreographed the elaborate ceremonies and music? Was it a group of straight guys that sat around a table and decided priests should wear pink vestments twice a year? A man said to me on Gaudete (*Rejoice*) Sunday, "Father, don't ever wear that on the street!"

55

No time for this!   Or this!

The Church couldn't function without gays any more than it could without women. The System has eliminated half of the human race (women) from the priesthood. The other half (men) are not standing in line to be celibate. The small piece of the pie that is left consists of those who choose to be celibate. What is their motivation? No one knows.

The argument for celibacy goes like this: "If priests were married they would have a wife and many children (no birth control!) They would be up nights with a sick child, changing diapers, worrying about how to support their children and how to afford Catholic schools. How would they get along with an outspoken wife with a mind of her own? They cannot be married because they must be available to

The Human Race

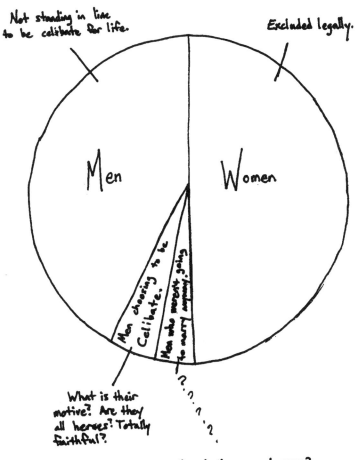

Not standing in line to be celibate for life.

Excluded legally.

Men

Women

Men choosing to be Celibate.

Men who weren't going to marry anyway.

What is their motive? Are they all heroes? Totally faithful?

? ? ? ?

Where's the normal curve?

What can we do about the shortage of Priests? ? ?

the customers twenty-four hours a day, every day! What???

They have administrative duties, meetings to attend, retreats twice a year, Masses, Baptisms, Weddings, Counseling and Confession. What a load! Besides it would be too expensive for the church to support men with wives and children. Now we're talking!

A fellow priest said to me, with a scotch in one hand and a cigar in the other, "The laity sucks; they don't understand what we go through. We have given up everything to follow Christ." I almost choked on my scotch. Words failed me; "bullshit" would not have sufficed!

Rome has forbidden discussion of the ordination of women; so I'm not discussing it; I'm just commenting! It is not apparent how women reflect the *"persona Christi."* In the Middle Ages they had the candidate for ordination raise his robes and sit on a stool with a hole in the middle of it, in order to see his testicles hanging through. If none were there, the ordination would be invalid. That criteria still holds today, it seems! Are we sure that all priests have testes? Do you have to have testes to resemble Christ?

Often during a lifeless homily, I have wished a woman I knew were up there preaching. People wouldn't be dozing.

Where did this plumbing theology come from? It sounds Freudian to me. Could this be a matter of power? You may not put much stock in Freud. Neither do I, but some of his symbolism fits pretty well! (See end note #4, Page 81.)

Many Catholics are now acting like grown people who think things through, and make their own decisions.

The deposit of faith is safe. No one has denied any dogma yet! It is *policies* that are being questioned! Not *de fide* teachings.

The church situation today sounds like Albert Camus' play, *The Plague*. In this story, there are dead rats every-

Could Freud be right?

Checking for credentials.

where in the town, but the city officials refuse to call it a plague. Everyone is left to deal with this "non-plague" individually. Camus describes how various characters lived their lives during the plague. Some take advantage of the suffering and make money on it. One man sits on his porch counting beans all day. A Jesuit priest in the pulpit blames the people, saying it is because of their sins! The doctor knows there is a plague and goes about the business of healing people! He finds meaning in his love for his wife and her love for him and in their love for people. He's the Christ figure.

The "town officials," the leaders of the church, do not

admit there is a Crisis in the Church. It is merely a passing phase. We have had many of them before! (See end note #5, Page 82.)

My Catholic education always started with answers, not questions. From Catechism through Theology I learned answers. All the happenings in the Universe were interpreted to agree with these answers. My ideals for myself and for the whole world were formed accordingly!

If you know your answers are irrefutable, you can use logic and history to make a case in favor of the answers you believe to be true. If you are dizzy, it's because of the circular thinking! Logic, when divorced from concrete facts, doesn't hold water.

Starting with answers often left me feeling very wise. Ministry contradicted that notion. Some answers were im-

possible to reconcile in everyday life. People said to me, "You always see connections and similarities and never the problems."

That was true. Problems interrupted my flow of thought! Experience has taught me that questions come first and then you find out how your answers fit, and you are ready to revise them. Sounds like Science. (See end note #6, Page 82.)

I accepted everything I was taught in Catholic school, despite some problems because I trusted my parents and teachers. I did not feel free to think for myself but couldn't

This won't work...

No See   No Hear   No Speak

No Problem!

help doing it! This did not help the maturing process. Seminary helped a little. *Being out among the people was where my second education began. I faced problems that forced me to think independently, and led me to where I am today.*

Seeing the anguish of married couples over the birth-control issue and couples going for years without the sacraments because their case had not been accepted by the marriage Tribunal made me angry and skeptical. These faithful people believed in all the dogmas at the Church but the interpretation of "rules" had separated them from the sacraments and caused misery. (See end note #7, Page 83.)

The clerical celibacy rule has not been revised since the eleventh century *when it was first enforced.* Perhaps it has never changed because priests did not discuss their problems with anyone except their Confessors. I have only my own experience to go on. I was tempted to leave many times. I saw fellow priests go through hell, drink excessively, become reclusive and miserable. All of this may not have been due to celibacy, but "mandated celibacy" does not make you a more loving person. At least ten of the best priests I have ever known left to get married. In recent years, four of the youngest priests in my Diocese have left to get married. Most of them would volunteer to celebrate Mass today if allowed; so would a number of those who left in the past.

VI
Conclusion (Close to the End)

I started this book with the thoughts of a child responding to religious instruction given by young nuns; then of a teenager taught by priests; then of a seminarian being taught how to think like a priest, and finally in active ministry of a priest facing real problems.

I hope to keep on growing in faith, hope and charity without the help of celibate lawmakers! I forgive them for torturing me for many years. May they rest in peace.

An important stage in growing up is recognizing that our parents are only human beings! That comes hard to most of us. After all, parents are our whole world when we are in the nest. They keep us safe and teach us how to live. We take what they tell us as truth whether we like it or not! When we find out *how* human they are it sometimes leads to disillusionment and rebellion. If we accept them, we can become their friends as adults. If they continue to treat us like children, we can tolerate it and love them, but go our own ways using our mature judgment. Growing up means becoming self-directed and productive. Growing up means *letting go.*

That's the way I feel about Mother Church. I still love Her despite disillusionment. When I found out my mother smoked secretly I was also disillusioned! I'm not surprised that the Church has secrets too!!

Jesus said, "The truth will set you free." Maybe the lawmakers need to be set free from their preoccupation with *control* and the *sexual lives* of the faithful. Laws of the Church have been changed before. They could be changed again.

The officials of the church have used capital punishment to subdue "heretics" in the past. The Inquisition investigated Teresa of Avila for twenty years. Thomas Aquinas was investigated while teaching at the University of Paris; Galileo has been pardoned, but professors still lose their positions at Catholic Universities if they are considered unorthodox. They have not been excommunicated—just intimidated by losing their livelihood! We have made *some* progress. (See end note #8, Page 84.)

If we have been set free by the Spirit of Jesus we don't need detailed laws and regulations to *control* us.

John XXIII was filled with the Spirit. He loved *all* of God's people, regardless of their religion or lack of religion. His Council was a miracle!

After his death, the Administrative Church gradually returned to a medieval structure that was built by historical events from Constantine 'til the Holy Roman Empire, which has had a history of control and force. The Holy Roman Empire *died*. The Church which formed that Empire has not died, but is still encrusted in the ancient structure which John XXIII had tried to reform. (See end note, #9, Page 85.)

Why did I write this book? Because I find life to be *a quest, a thirst, a longing.*

Aquinas said, "We know what God is *not*, rather than what God is." *Quid est Deus?* What is God? That was why he wrote. He was seeking God. He wrote a book of questions, not answers to end the search!

My novice master said, "You did not come here to *find* God, but to *seek* God." The presence of mystery evokes quest.

Am I angry? Yes. I'm pissed at people who have all the

answers! I'm angry at the squelchers of hungry minds and hearts. I don't hate them or condemn them. I just keep traveling and don't let them stop me on my quest. They are searching too, aren't they?

I wrote this book because I had to vent my frustration and my hope for a new day in the Church I have served so long.

I hope my words have not shaken anyone's faith. They may have offended some of you. These words are tendentious because I have a definite point of view. That point of view has been shaped by forty-eight years in the priesthood, serving and loving people and it is offered with honesty.

My journey will be over soon. I'm on a quest till then!

VII
X-Rated Section

You should not read this section if you are easily offended by discussing subjects that involve sex, or if you are convinced that all teachings in that area are infallible teachings and not the products of "celibate moral theologians." Wait 'til you hear some of them! It was difficult to think up suitable cartoons for this section!!

Natural law was developed by Thomas Aquinas, based on Aristotle. Natural law has been applied mostly to the *reproductive powers.*

The sexual organs were intended by nature for the procreation of the race. The natural function of sex can never be blocked by contraception of any kind except by abstaining from sex during the fertile period each month, (If you know when it is). Isn't that frustrating the purpose of sex? A woman once confessed committing adultery and added she used birth control. The priest said the adultery was a serious sin but the birth control was a good idea.

If a couple is using natural family planning they may sleep together but not have sex during the fertile period. This interpretation of natural law was written by a celibate who sleeps single in a single bed!

Now let's apply natural law to other functions, just for fun.

Saliva was intended by nature to lubricate ingested food and break down starches.

<u>Logical conclusion.</u> Saliva was not intended for licking stamps, spitting on the ground or thumb sucking.

Fact: The eye has a natural appetite for light.

Question: Are sun glasses permitted?

Fact: The ear has a natural appetite for sound.

Question: Are ear plugs permitted?

Fact: The brain has a natural appetite for thinking.

Question: What about impure thoughts?

Question: Is every sex act supposed to be open to procreation? YES.

Question: If that law were followed literally wouldn't we be smothering in babies?

Question: Is masturbation always a mortal sin? YES.

Question: Even in giving a specimen for a fertility check.
Answer: If a married man needs one, it must be done with a needle. OUCH! (Celibates don't need such tests!)

Question: Is masturbation against the natural law?
Answer: YES. So it's unnatural? Yes, but not rare.

Question: Is homosexuality intrinsically disordered?
Answer: It is not intrinsically disordered to be homosexual, but it is sinful to commit sexual acts if you are homosexual!

Question: What is the natural function of the sex organs of homosexuals?
Answer: Strictly for the elimination of urine!

Question: Would gay people be allowed to be married if they promised to be celibate?
Answer: No, they would not be able to perform the marriage act.
Response: Oh, so that's what constitutes marriage!

Fact: Clerical celibacy frustrates the purpose of the sexual organs, but is not "unnatural." It is "supernatural." It enables priests to love everyone while loving no one (i.e., sexually). A priest friend once said, "For me, the only joy of celibacy is the hiss of my piss without a miss."

Fact: Diocesan priests have *NO VOWS*. They have a *promise* of obedience to the Bishop which includes the promise of celibacy! (Look it up!)

Fact: One priest said, "Whenever I slip up on my promise of celibacy, I just go to confession and say, I disobeyed the Bishop once and I committed one sin of impurity. That covers it."

Question: Was he right?
Answer: Not morally, but legally he was! Neither person was married so it wasn't adultery—just a grave sin against purity.

Question: Is every divorced person supposed to be celibate?

Answer: Yes, until the Tribunal of the church has investigated every nook and cranny of their personal lives and concluded there was something radically wrong with their first marriage!

Response: They already knew that!! Why don't they take your word for it? They had to find out if it violated Canon Law!!!

Question: Who is the Tribunal?

Answer: A priest with a degree in Canon Law. Several priests for judges who don't have to have a degree in Canon Law; several ladies (usually) who review cases (discuss them with each other!) and prepare them for the Judges. The ladies are paid for their services, along with typists who type up the documents. In the local Tribunal these people sometimes know the person who is appealing for a decree of nullity. But they are forbidden to discuss cases outside the office. So don't worry.

Question: Is divorce and remarriage against Canon Law?

Answer: No, it's against Divine Law. Thank God for Canon lawyers who can find loopholes even here!

Question: Could it be that the consciences of the two people seeking an annulment are the ultimate Tribunal? Could it be that they themselves are in a better position to solve their consciences than the celibate Canon lawyers and the lady investigators? Is that heretical thinking?

Question: What if you lie and make up stories in your paperwork, coach your witnesses, and consult someone who knows what the Canon lawyers are looking for? Your case goes through with flying colors. That's entirely possible! Do you need confession before receiving Holy Communion? Do you confess this specific lie, or just mention "a lie"?

Question: What if you are perfectly sincere and honest in answering all questions and your witnesses are not coached and then your case is rejected? Can you go to confession and talk it over with a priest, resolve your conscience and then continue receiving Holy Communion?
Answer: YES, it's called the INTERNAL FORUM. Not many Catholics know this! The Tribunal staff does not attach a note to that effect when it sends out a rejection notice; that's for you to find out! (I, personally, think all marriage case are subjects for the Internal Forum where matters of conscience are resolved, not matters of legality.)

Dirty thoughts while writing

Moral Theology!

Why did the moral theologians write all this? Was it a fixation on sex? Or was it lust for control of others, or both? A friend once said to me, "If you can control the most intimate and personal realm of a person's life, you have complete control over that person." That was the best explanation I have ever heard! The Church must get control of these unruly humans. But in such detail? Is it necessary to legislate every aspect of life for mature responsible human beings who are struggling to live the spirit of Christ?

NOTE: When you thought your parish priest was crazy, he was really just a true believer in the Moral Theology he was taught in the Seminary! I personally believed all this stuff as a young man! It was after *I grew up* and lived among "normal" people that I realized it was *nonsense.*

Justice, fairness, respect, faithfulness, and honesty were not treated nearly so extensively! It must be hard to make detailed laws in these areas, and biological moral theologians didn't dwell on such subjects—period.

Thank God we have new moral theologians today, but they are under suspicion. Young priests are still being taught the "same stuff" mentioned here. They will have to re-educate themselves.

Contemporary moral theologians depart from this old kind of morality and focus on the human dimensions of moral actions and the intent of God's law.

I want to quote one of these theologians, Dick Westley, who writes so powerfully: "The primary function of any Christian community is to be a group of people who accept others and who help others to accept themselves, *no matter what they have done.* The world in its best moments wants peace and reconciliation, and every sincere person in the world wants acceptance and pardon. The Christian Church is called by God to be explicitly what the world implicitly wants: a community in which mutual acceptance and forgiveness are a reality. The loses of midlife reveal the human condition better than anything else. One becomes sensitized to the burdens others carry. Trapped in prisons not of their own choosing, suffering untold pain, one's heart begins to expand to embrace them all. The focus of one's love goes out beyond the family, beyond immediate friends to all who share with us the human condition. Compassion for the whole of humankind overwhelms one's soul. At such times, one cries out in hopeful love the words of *Godspell:* 'When will God save the people? O God of Mercy—when?' And suddenly, one feels called not only to morality, but to its beyond.

Adolescence, young adulthood, mid-life and old age each contains a new lesson to be learned, a new skill at being spirit, a new challenge to be moral. It is new and yet it is the same because at each stage we are asked to do the same work of spirit, but only in different circumstances. All of this becomes clear if only we give heed to our lives and live long enough."

VIII
End Notes

End Note #1

From page 39: *Church History*
A short overview of Church history which is very read-able can be found in Thomas Cahill's small book, *John XXIII.* Cahill discusses all the popes up to John XXIII. He covers the most significant crises in the Church. It is short and very en-joyable and can be purchased at your local bookstore:

The Penguin Group
Penguin Putman, Inc.
345 Hudson Street
New York, NY 10014

End Note #2

From page 48: *Reserved Sins*
Many Catholics have never heard of a "reserved sin." The Catholic Church used to make abortion a "reserved sin." I don't think it still does today. Here is how the term is explained in the *Catholic Encyclopedia:*
"A term used for sins whose absolution is not within the power of every confessor, but is reserved to himself by

78

the superior of the confessor, or only specially granted to some other confessor by that superior. To reserve a case is then to refuse jurisdiction for the absolution of a certain sin. Christ gave power to the rulers of His Church to make such reservations: 'Whose sins you shall retain they are retained' (John's Gospel, chapter xx, vs. 23). The reservation of sins presupposes jurisdiction, and therefore the Pope alone can make reservation for the whole Church; bishops can do the same for their diocese only and certain regular prelates for their religious subjects. That a sin be reserved it must be mortal, external, and consummated. If a sin be reserved in one diocese, and if a penitent, without the intention of evading the law, confesses to a priest in another diocese where the sin is not reserved, the latter may absolve the reserved sin. Cases are reserved either

- merely on account of the sin itself, that is without censure, or
- on account of the censure attached to it.

If a penitent be in danger of death, any priest can absolve him, both from reserved censures and reserved sins. In case of reserved censures, if he recovers, he must later present himself to the one having special power for reserved censures, unless the case was simply reserved to the Pope. As to reserved sins, he need not, as a general rule, present himself again after convalescence. In a case of urgent necessity, when it is not possible to have recourse to the proper superior, an ordinary priest may absolve a penitent, directly from unreserved sins and indirectly from Episcopal reserved cases, but the penitent must afterwards apply to the person having power to absolve from the reservation. If there were also papal reservations, either simple or special, the absolution is direct, but in case of special reservations to the Pope a relation must be made to the *Holy See* that its mandates on the subject may be obtained. Ignorance of a censure prevents its being incurred but moralists dispute whether ignorance of a reservation, with or without censure, excuses from its incurrence. If it be a case with censure reserved to the Pope, all agree that ignorance does excuse from it; reserved to a bishop, it is controverted. Some moralists hold that ignorance excuses from all reservations, whether with or without censure. It is certain, however, that a bishop has authority to declare that ignorance of a reservation does not prevent its incurrence in his diocese."

This is an example of how Canon Law speaks!!!!!

End Note #3

From page 55: Dick Westley, *Morality and Its Beyond*, Page 35 (in his book)

Here is how a contemporary moral theologian, Dick Westley, speaks on birth control:

> Whenever and under whatever circumstances a human person is deprived of what is needed for life and human development, we are face to face with ontic evil ("ontic" refers to basic evil in reality). *Moral evil always involves an unjustified infliction of ontic evil. The free, deliberate, and unjustified intention and/or action of inflicting ontic evil on oneself or others.* One important consequence of this is that nothing is immoral simply because someone in authority says so. It is because something is immoral that authority forbids it. But authoritative prohibition by itself is never sufficient reason to judge something to be immoral. Contraceptive love-making between spouses may or may not be morally evil. In the case of contraception, for example, to prohibit it is to deprive spouses of the pleasure of engaging in sexual actions with

peace of mind, which means the prohibition itself inflicts an ontic evil. That means that the prohibition itself is going to have to be justified.

Evil comes from basically good people like us, whose hunger for more of the good of life for ourselves causes us to rationalize the infliction of ontic evil on others.

The problem is that truth has to be experienced and personally appropriated somehow. It cannot be proven, or taught to others by simply telling them what it is; it must be personally experienced if it is to be known at all. And what is that truth? It is that human persons are precious, unique, and worth suffering or undergoing ontic evil for. It is the sort of truth one knows only by "feeling" it. Of course, feeling it is not enough; I must then act upon it. This means I must so conduct myself so as to show that each human life is precious, unique, and unprecedented, and I will resist *all* attempts to reduce it or gamble away its inherent meaning. In the absence of that experience, all moral cogitations become either empty rationalizations, or self-seeking sophistries.

End Note #4

From page 58: *Freudian Symbolsim*

The big hat and the crozier could be interpreted as phallic symbols in Freudian terms. Certainly they are symbols of power. They impress me as arrogant, pretentious and out of date by centuries!!

End Note #5

From page 61: *Crises in the Church*

In chapter two of *The Political Vision of the Divine Comedy*, Joan Ferrante says: "Perhaps the best known of Boniface VIII's authentic statements is the bull, *Unam Sanctam*, 1302 A.D., claiming a divine hierarchy in which spiritual power excels any earthly power in dignity and nobility and establishing the earthly power; the spiritual power can judge the earthly, whereas only God can judge the spiritual. Anyone who does not accept the Pope's position is a heretic, and it is essential to the salvation of any human creature to be subject to the Roman Pontiff."

How's that for problem solving? I don't think it would work today!

End Note #6

From page 62: *Church and Science*

Science starts with questions and seeks possible explanations for physical phenomena. The Church, which starts with answers to all the deepest questions of life, often finds itself in conflict with scientists like Galileo, and philosophers of all sorts. The Church has resorted to "condemnation" too often. The Church is not qualified to judge scientific findings per se and philosophers are free to express their thinking. It is embarrassing to many Catholics to have statements from the Vatican on Science.

The latest statement on condoms not being a solution to the AIDS crisis was particularly embarrassing, since no one had ever said it was a solution.

End Note #7

From page 64: Hans Küng,
My Struggle for Freedom, Page 324 (in his book)

> Unlike his great predecessor, John XXIII didn't want to be a great churchman, orator, diplomat, scholar and organizer, as he already said in his coronation address. Just a good shepherd. Following the example of the biblical Peter, he wanted to comfort, strengthen and motivate his brothers and sisters. The more time went on, the more he proved his greatness in serving; here he had the backing of the words of another who makes his greatness unassailable 'Whoever among you will be the greatest, let him be your servant.' He didn't simply teach a new papacy but lived it out, and precisely in so doing introduced an epoch-making paradigm shift for the papacy: instead of an absolutist Roman primacy of rule, as had been the practice from the time of Gregory VII and Innocent III to Pius IX to Pius XII, a pastoral primacy of service. A papacy with a human, Christian face.

My Struggle for Freedom, Page 306 (in his book)

> But in the threat to freedom in the church from within, Christians can find protection, refuge and freedom only in solitude within themselves—in the refuge of their free consciences.
>
> Here I am by no means thinking only of extreme cases like Galileo and John of the Cross in the prison of the Inquisition, or Joan of Arc at the stake. I am also thinking of the countless scientists, philosophers, theologians, politicians, known and unknown, who have been involved in severe conflicts of conscience—why? Because representatives of the church didn't keep to the boundaries set for them by the freedom of all the children of God. Because they confused God's revelation with an ideology. Because they exceeded

their competences and involved themselves in pure questions of science, philosophy, politics and economics. It is infinitely tragic that particularly in modern times countless people have fled from the Church, the original sphere of freedom, to seek freedom in the world. Here only one thing is of any use: more than ever, the Church today, where freedom is threatened so severely from outside and from within, must try once again to be a truly hospitable home in freedom for all those who are well-disposed to it. Certainly capriciousness shouldn't prevail in the church, but ordered freedom. But the *manifestations of freedom in the Church mustn't be suppressed.* That begins with the freedom of conscience which is so often scorned and condemned; it is first recognized unambiguously by John XXIII in his encyclical *Pacem in Terris* and, I say clearly, holds even in the face of dogma, which must never be accepted if it goes against the conscience.

Freedom in the Church is not a theory; freedom in the Church is a *reality and a challenge.* How much freedom shall be made real in the Church depends—on you, on me, on all of us.

End Note #8

From page 67: Hans Küng,
My Struggles for Freedom, page 365 (of his book)

> It is evident that the church magisterium has very great difficulties in publicly conceding errors of whatever kind, although such errors are known to any well informed Catholic: from the condemnation of Galileo and the Chinese name for God and rites through the condemnation of freedom of religion, human rights and the doctrine of evolution, to all the historically erroneous decrees of the Biblical Commission under Pius X. The Vatican doesn't err!

End Note #9

From page 67: Eugene Kennedy,
The Unhealed Wound, Page 41 (of his book)

Officials cut scholars off from the universe of their genera-
tion by ousting them from academic faculties, forbidding
them to write or speak on the subject of their expertise, and
insisting on their accepting and keeping silent about
changes in their creative work authored and imposed by
others. Sometimes they are told, as the Swiss scholar Hans
Kung and the American moralist Charles Curran were, that
they can no longer call themselves *Catholic* theologians. That
the sexuality at the core of this "Galileo Myth" is manipula-
tive, unhealthy and exploitive may be read in the debase-
ment, humiliation and shaming that characterize it.